Coincidental Pursuit
Searching for My Birth Parents

By Beverly Hendrix

Copyright © 2016
By Beverly Hendrix
Published By NorTex Press
An Imprint of Wild Horse Media Group
P.O. Box 331779
Fort Worth, Texas 76163
1-817-344-7036
www.WildHorseMedia.com
ALL RIGHTS RESERVED
1 2 3 4 5 6 7 8 9
ISBN-10: 1-68179-035-1
ISBN-13: 978-1-68179-035-0

Author Website
www.BeverlyHendrix.com

Legacy of an Adopted Child

Once there were two women
Who never knew each other.
One you do not remember
The other you call mother.

Two different lives
Shaped to make your one.
One became your guiding star,
The other became your sun.

The first gave you life
And the second taught you to live in it.
The first gave you a need for love
And the second was there to give it.

One gave you a nationality,
The other gave you a name.
One gave you the seed of talent,
The other gave you an aim.

One gave you emotions,
The other calmed your fears.
One saw your first sweet smile,
The other dried your tears.

One gave you up –
It was all that she could do.
The other prayed for a child
And God led her straight to you.

And now you ask me
Through your tears,
The age-old question
Through the years:

Heredity or environment –
Which are you the product of?
Neither, my darling – neither,
Just two different kinds of love

Author Unknown

*This book is dedicated to my mother,
Betty Guthrie Bowden,
for giving me the inspiration to put my
incredible journey of searching for my roots
into words. I thank her for always supporting
my sense of curiosity.*

Table of Contents

Acknowledgments i
Preface ii
Introduction: Meaningful Coincidences iv
Chapter 1: The Beginning 1
Chapter 2: The Accident 5
Chapter 3: College and After 11
Chapter 4: The Letter 14
Chapter 5: Searching for Stacia 17
Chapter 6: The Stall 21
Chapter 7: The Nail Salon 23
Chapter 8: The Reunion 37
Chapter 9: The Search for My Father 43
Chapter 10: Making Contact . . . Again 46
Chapter 11: A Marriage, a Birth, and a Death 50
Chapter 12: Another Happy Beginning 53
Chapter 13: Finding – and Losing – Bruce 55
Chapter 14: Kinship and Friendship 57
Chapter 15: Reflections on Who I Am 60
About the Author 67

Acknowledgments

I would like to thank my adoptive parents, Ben and Betty Bowden, for giving me such a wonderful opportunity at life. Such a love story is theirs, and it is one I never tire of hearing. They met at Baylor Hospital in Dallas, Texas. He was a doctor starting out in Dallas after serving in the war in Korea; she was a talented nurse. A more loving, generous, and kind couple would be hard to find. They were married sixty years, and it only ended when she lost him to Alzheimer's in 2009.

My mother is a thriving eighty-eight-year old at the time of this writing and rivals many who are years younger than she in her open-minded thinking, professionalism, civic duties, and social activities. "Thank you" seems hardly big enough, but I do, for empowering me with all of the tools needed to be successful and happy.

Ben and Betty Bowden 1948

> "I think, at a child's birth, if a mother could
> ask a fairy godmother to endow it with the most
> useful gift, that gift would be curiosity"
>   -- Eleanor Roosevelt

Preface

My story is an accounting of my life and of the five years (1985 to 1989) I spent searching for my biological parents. I reveal the what, the where, and the many whens that took place and how I accomplished this.

The journey threw me headfirst into a world I was not familiar with. I will explain the twists, turns, failures, victories, and most everything else that went on in between while searching for my biological parents and try to explain why coincidence and curiosity showed me the way. There is no greater gift than the answers uncovered by a curious mind.

> *"When you live your life with an appreciation of coincidences and their meanings, you connect with the underlying field of infinite possibilities."*
> -- Deepak Chopra

Introduction: Meaningful Coincidences

COINCIDENCE [koh- in-si–duh ns]
1. A striking occurrence of two or more events at one time apparently by mere chance: *Our meeting in Venice was pure coincidence.*

PURSUIT [per–soot]
1. An activity that you spend time and energy doing: *the pursuit of happiness.*

We are all born into this world of some circumstance, this I know to be true. Through the ages, however, by whatever circumstances determine our impending arrival and whether or not the birth is planned, accidental, or through Immaculate Conception, society has always dictated certain rules as to how the new bundle of joy is accepted.

In the 1950s, the decade of my birth, unwed and pregnant were two coinciding events that were not well received. I am a product of that era. This is the chronological story of my life and how and why I chose, as an adopted child, to search for my birth parents. I express what I learned along the way, and how it changed my life. I will share with you my journey and why I chose to call it my **Coincidental Pursuit**.

Chapter 1

The Beginning

My name is Beverly Hendrix. I go by many names: Beverly, Bev, B.J., and Bevo to many. You can also call me fortunate because I received a precious gift at my birth. I was adopted at three days old to Dr. Ben and Betty Bowden of Dallas in April 1956.

My life was shaped by a decision three people made years ago. It is not my intention to judge, praise, criticize, or influence anyone in any way. I simply wanted to put my story into words as a reflection of the many coincidental events that got me here and made me who I am. The details in this writing are all true. My birth mother's name has been changed at her request for privacy issues.

I have always known, at least as far back as my memory goes, that I was adopted at birth. My parents told me a story about a woman who had a baby but was unable to care for the infant. Ben and Betty wanted a baby so badly and they were able to take care of the child. It was that simple. I thought that was perfectly normal. Being adopted was something that I was taught to be proud of and being so made me feel special. When I was very young and having a child's mind, I thought that being adopted and being left handed put me in a rather elite group. For example, on one occasion when very young, I recall being in the Sunday school kitchen where little children played during "big church." The children were to take turns using the pretend oven, but I wanted and felt entitled to continue my play time longer than my allotted turn. I based that extension and entitlement of playtime vocally by telling my friend about my "special" qualities." I actually told one little girl that I was special because I was an adopted child . . . and left handed, and, therefore, was entitled to more play time on the oven. I recall a nice woman coming over and calmly, but firmly, explaining to me that albeit my argument was a good one, it was not to be used in the wrong way. I was embarrassed by the reprimand and learned a valuable lesson of humility that day.

Occasionally, when I was very young I would have a sort of dream. It would take over just before sleep when I was in a dream-like state. I would lie in bed at night and very vividly try to remember what I thought must have happened when a child was adopted. I would squint my eyes to shield them from the bright lights that surely must have been overhead illuminating all of the babies needing homes. The lights above each crib were there to highlight us for all of the "prospective parent people" browsing the many rows of baby beds in the big warehouse-type store, enabling them to see us clearly. I suppose I formulated the concept for "Babies R Us" before they did. Rows and rows of babies were just waiting for some nice people to pick them. The place was huge. I would think that I must have been a good, quiet baby with a smile—yes, that's what it took to get picked. Lucky me! I did not have to stay there any longer. Funny how little minds work, but that was very real to me. It appeared to be such a simple process, kind of like a cafeteria of unwanted babies. You would go there, shop, select your baby, and then go home to happy ever after. A brilliant and uncomplicated concept!

My parents adopted my older brother four years before my adoption, giving me my first brother, Barry. All was well. They later adopted another son three years my junior. Brother number two, Brian, was welcomed into the fold. Little did they know, however, that within a few years my mother would give birth to another brother, Brad, then eleven months later, yet another brother, Blake. Brothers three and four were here. Oh my, four boys and a girl. I considered myself in a pretty good spot.

My entire family's first names started with the letter "B," even Mom and Dad's. It seemed a pattern was evolving, seven family members whose names all began with the letter "B"—Ben, Betty, Barry, Beverly, Brian, Brad, and Blake—and a dog that would come along later my father would name Brunhilda. We all shared the same initials of BB. It became quite confusing at times.

In addition to being a general practitioner (his day job), my father raised Charolais cattle and some horses on our farm in Kaufman County, Texas. We had eight hundred beautiful acres he fenced, worked, and manicured. Some wonderful memories were made there and that is where my love of horses was born. My father chose to incorporate his cattle brand as 7B, for the seven Bowdens. My parents swear that cornering the market using the letter "B," a/k/a the "B" fest, was not planned, but the jury is still out on that one.

I had an ideal childhood. My father was a very well respected doctor in Dallas. The words kind, compassionate, fair, and honest best describe him. He also had a musical gift and had an incredible ear for music. Even in his last years when Alzheimer's robbed him of his memory of most everything else, he still held onto the gift of playing the piano and entertained all of the residents on a daily basis in the retirement home where he lived. He passed away in 2009 but his legacy lives on. He is credited with delivering about half of my high school graduating class. My senior class was comprised of 999 students, which would calculate out to be a significant number of deliveries he took part in. He touched many lives in such a positive way. I recently attended my fortieth high school reunion and was touched by so many wonderful stories my classmates shared with me about what he meant to their families. My father is greatly missed.

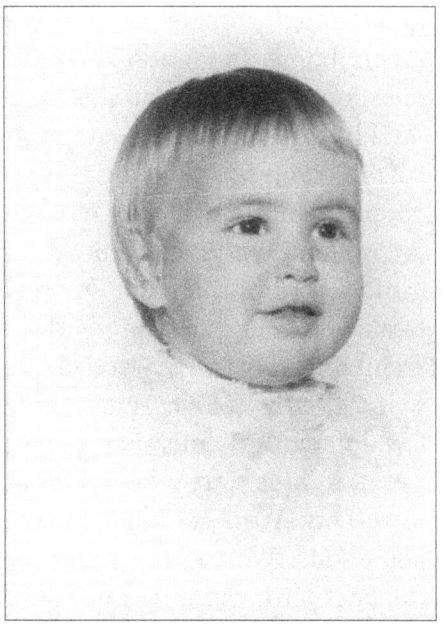

Bev - 1957

My mother is often compared to the actress Donna Reed, best known for her role in the Christmas classic *It's a Wonderful Life*, in looks and actions. I don't know how my mother managed five children, but she did it with a stern hand, grace, poise, and a whole lot of fun. She once brought a goat home as a pet for our suburban backyard in Dallas—priceless! There are not words enough to explain the gratitude and love I feel toward my parents.

I only now realize the selfless attitude of all parties involved—meaning, of course, my wonderful parents and how selfless one must be to adopt a child, but also to my birth mother, as you also have to be selfless to give up a child. I did not always feel this way and herein lies the problem with adoption. Even in the best situation, and even though you know how fortunate you are to have been born and received into a loving home, in an adopted child's mind there is always that nagging question. It is subtle, but it is there: Why did they not want me?

I like to think of the adoption process as a "big roll of the dice." All parties involved are taking a huge gamble on what kind of children they adopt. Then again, having biological children is also a huge gamble.

My family was a "blended family" before blended family even became a common term. Remarkably, though, I never remember being treated or feeling any differently than the two biological sons. I never felt an inkling of bias. We were all as individuals, and as a group, treated the same. This, of course, is my remembrance; all or some of the boys may feel differently. Remember, I was the only girl. We were one big unit. The five of us kids were a twenty-four hour, seven-day a week, buzzing hive of activity. We were loud, hungry, sticky, active children just enjoying being kids. We covered miles on our bicycles, built countless forts in the backyard, claiming a record for the biggest Christmas tree fort in the history of my neighborhood by using seventy-five plus Christmas trees we gathered off front lawns from miles around. We would send out the scouts (younger kids) and they would return dragging them behind their bikes. I am still in awe at how we pulled that off. We water skied, rode horses, and traveled to Yellowstone National Park in a travel trailer, for heaven's sake. Lunch would be sandwiches on the side of the road. Totally terrific!

I love all of those memories. I could not, however, predict how quickly my idyllic life was about to change—and how much I would learn from it.

Betty With Her Five Kids - 1963

Chapter 2

The Accident

My teen years were active. Church softball, school, tons of friends, riding my horse with my sweet friend Ann and her sisters all over Flag Pole Hill. It was wonderful. I have such happy memories of those days. Riding bareback, we would stop and lie back on our horses and just stare at the sky. I can still feel the sun on my face when I reminisce about those days in our early teens and recall our serious conversations about what we would become as adults, what our futures might be like, and who would we marry? I treasure the innocence and simplicity of that time and the happy memories.

When I was fifteen I was invited by a family friend to attend a Moody Blues concert in Fort Worth. It was April 3, 1972—a day that changed my life. My first date—well, kind of. I was so excited!

While traveling to the concert we were involved in a terrible car accident on the Fort Worth Turnpike. I was riding in the back seat. We were hit from behind while at a complete stop at one of the tollbooths by a car traveling at an excessive speed; I do not believe that he ever even attempted to stop. I have no recollection of the horrible event, nor the day before, and I was seriously injured in the accident. I broke the femur bone in my right leg and sustained many bumps, bruises, and lacerations. I have small snippets of memory of the paramedics cutting my shirt off. My mother had just made the trendy styled "peasant top" for me and I remember thinking, "Oh no, no, don't cut it!" As I said, I remember very little until waking up in Baylor Hospital after a long surgery to set my leg in traction. A screw was inserted horizontally through my tibia and then cables suspended weights that hung off the end of the bed. This pulled the bone and allowed it to align properly. All of this rigging was housed around me in an engineering feat of metal bars and screws. The treatment was very high tech for 1972.

I would ask repeatedly what had happened to me. Losing any memory of an event is very disturbing. It still bothers me all of these many years later. The human body is an amazing machine, so fragile on the one hand and then so strong on the other, meaning the remarkable ability to block a painful and traumatic event from memory. I remained in traction in the hospital for eight weeks. The bone did not want to "knit," or heal properly during the first few weeks and the doctors were very concerned. It was a very frightening time for me. I was force-fed protein and my bone finally began to heal. At fifteen, eight weeks is an eternity, but friends and family were incredibly supportive. Every time I smell that "hospital smell" I am reminded of this time in my life, and how lucky I was to come out of the whole situation with so few scars inside and out.

Looking back, I wish I had kept some kind of record of exactly how many games of Spades were played in that hospital bed. Friends and family would take shifts, it seemed. I was so bored! I am convinced that I broke a record in 1972 for the dirtiest hair ever. My hair was very long and could not be washed because of the traction rigging. I had to remain still, with no side-to-side movement for twenty-nine days. My mother had removed the shards of glass, but it was still gross. To this day I stay as far away as I can from a can of "dry" shampoo.

During my long hospital stay, I learned to type or "keyboard." Mom took a piece of cardboard and drew the keys on it. I would tilt it up on my stomach and I began to memorize the keyboard. Through various texts I taught myself proper hand placement, numbers, and so forth. I would practice sentences and numbers for hours. It was a productive way to pass the time. I had instant portable keyboarding and a "laptop" before it was even thought of.

I also taught myself to do embroidery work and began to embroider cute little flowers and other designs on denim work shirts. In no time the chair beside the hospital bed was stacked full of these shirts that classmates had brought to me. There was always another denim shirt just waiting to be worked on. I remember the feel of the denim and how hard it was to push the needle and thread through the thick fabric, causing sore fingers, but this creative outlet was so freeing to me at the time. The seed to my creative side was planted. I still love to be creative and may never have realized it if not for the accident. I thank my classmates for their role in "trying to keep me busy." Years later, the owner of one of the embroidered denim shirts told me she still had hers, albeit threadbare and so very fragile. Sharon, thank you for sharing that with me. I was touched.

I endured twenty-eight roommates during my incarceration in the hospital. Admitted and released, they would come and go for various medical procedures—just "short-timers" I called them. I did, however, receive a special roommate on April 24 named Karen. Karen was having knee surgery on both knees at the same time. I remember her so well because in talking we discovered that we shared the same birthday. We both would turn sixteen on April 26. What a coincidence! Our mothers got together and planned a surprise party for us with a big cake, friends, balloons, the works. It was awesome and a welcome break in the daily routine. The *Dallas Morning News* even showed up to do a story on the two unfortunate hospital bound sixteen-year-olds who shared a birthday and were stuck in the hospital when all they really wanted to be doing was standing in line at the Department of Public Safety to get their drivers licenses. The party was a wonderful break in the daily hospital routine. I thank everyone who was involved for that day, including three very special classmates: Don, Allen, and Russell who brought me a six-foot-tall teddy bear and laid him face down on top of the metal traction rigging of my hospital bed so he was looking down at me 24/7. He was quite the talk of the eighth floor. I named that bear DAR from the first

Car Accident - April 1972

letter of each of their names and kept it for years. Thanks, guys.

My recovery was a long and slow process that caused me to miss the end of my sophomore and the majority of my junior year at Bryan Adams High School in Dallas, Texas. My education was continued through a tutoring program called "Homebound" by tutors that came to the hospital and then later tutored me in my home so that I would not fall behind.

I was angry at that time with my father for choosing the recovery route that he did. In 1972, there were two options for the treatment of a broken femur: one was to have a twelve-inch metal rod inserted surgically to pin and stabilize the break reducing the "down time" to about three weeks; the second one was to endure eight weeks in traction, three months in a body cast, six weeks in a wheelchair, then a stint on crutches. Dad told me that his decision for the second option was based on the risk of infection with a surgical opening, and also that he did not want me to have a long ugly scar the entire length of my right thigh for the rest of my life. I know that the procedure today is done with a one-inch- long

The Accident

opening on the thigh. Timing is everything, right? Again, at my age I did not understand the significance of the wise choice he made. Thanks again, Daddy. As an adult, I now realize the wisdom in the decision and appreciate what he did for me.

So I endured a body cast, ribs to toes, for three months after traction—and no, I will not go into details on the question I was always asked: "How do you . . . you know, use the bathroom?" Don't even ask. Three months in a wheelchair, then a long stretch on crutches. No weight on my right leg for three months. I became quite good at one-legged showers.

This unfortunate event in my life taught me so much at an early age. I became more keenly aware of my own mortality and knew how fragile and strong the human body is. I was empowered with a more finely honed sense about the people and events that go on around us in our daily lives. We all take so much for granted in life. I became more aware and grateful for the present and saw people differently than before the accident. I learned that whether it was through a person's kind word, action, or even an encouraging smile, I was different. I saw and experienced firsthand what those simple actions had done for me during a

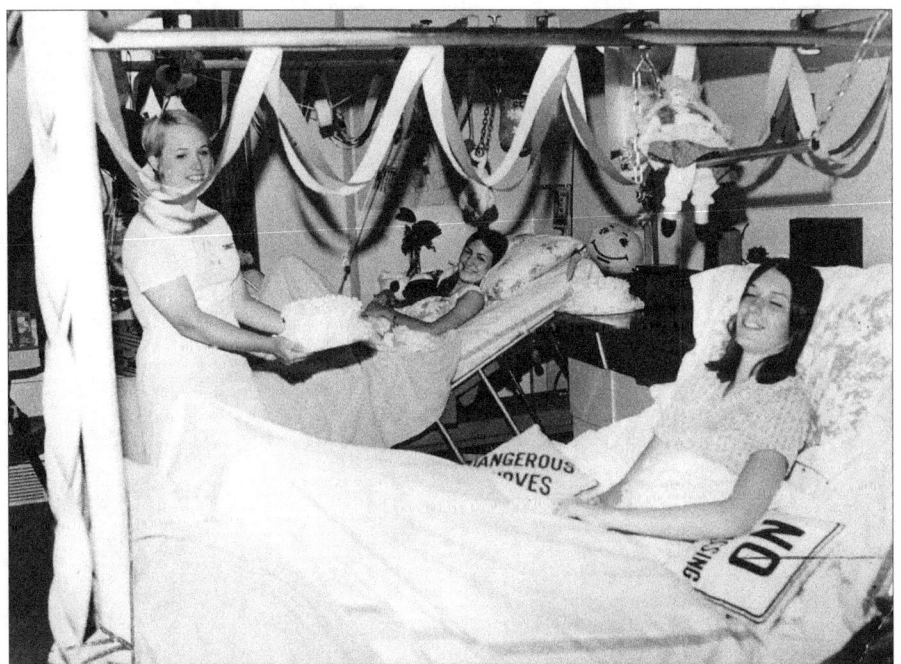

Bev and Roommate both turning 16 in Baylor Hospital on April 26, 1972.

challenging time and decided then that I wanted to be the one to give an encouraging word or smile to someone whenever I could. Small acts of kindness can mean so much. I try to practice this everyday.

I was never angry at anyone about the accident. It was just that, an accident. However, I learned early that a single event could change the rest of your life. With such a wonderful support system of family and friends and doctors, I overcame great obstacles, mostly unscathed, but with many scars that are constant reminders of this time in my life. The scars on my body are like personal tattoos, they make me unique and I embrace this. These lessons would serve me well in my future; I just didn't realize it yet.

Bev - Age 16

1974 Graduation

Chapter 3
College and After

I fully recovered from my injuries and graduated from high school on schedule in 1974. I then went on to earn my degree in merchandising and marketing from the University of North Texas (back then known as North Texas State University). It was a wonderful experience and I made some lifelong friends. I truly loved college and all that went with it. I made new friends and worked hard at getting my degree. I again am humbled by being surrounded by a network of incredible people who continue to touch my life in so many ways. I love you guys—you know who you are.

During my college years being adopted would come up in conversation from time to time, some people knew, some did not. It was not something that I dwelled upon; it was just a part of me.

I remember a speech class event that shook me to my core. We were divided into two groups and our topic of discussion was to be about the abortion issue in the 1970s. One group would debate the pro-life side; the other group would discuss the issue from the pro-choice perspective.

It was to be held as a debate. We did not pick our sides, the professor simply divided the room into two halves. Well, I was on the pro-choice side.

We all did our research and the debate went well. After the debate had ended and class was over a guy that I knew, but not very well, that had been on the opposing side from me during the debate ran up to me as I was walking on campus and said, "Hey Bev, why didn't you ask the professor to put you on the pro-life side of the room, seeing as you were adopted?" I had no idea he knew that I was adopted, or why he would say something like that to me. Perhaps he thought that I automatically was against abortion because of my beginning. It made me stop and question everything. It dawned on me for the first time that people may "assume" many things about me that may or may not be true—based on my being an adopted child. I had never considered this before and it made me begin to wonder about my heritage again.

After college graduation in 1978 I went to work for a high-end women's clothing manufacturer in Dallas. I loved the job and made a life-long friend there, Jamey Wolf. She has and will continue to be my inspiration, always. We have been through so much together. She is my confidant, my sounding board, interior decorator, and so much more. Jamey is always there at the end of the day for me and I cherish her friendship. She has an impeccable eye and fabulous taste. I find her to be the constant one in my life who is always honest and supportive. I absolutely love the way she looks at life and I am so fortunate to have her in mine. I believe it was her mother who once told me "we were cut from the same cloth." I liked that. She is the sister I never had.

I was married in 1981 for a short time. It did not work out. I learned the hard way that not all men were as sweet, loving and kind as my daddy. Our marriage had some major issues and we chose to end it amicably after two years. I had made a big mistake—but I was young and after "licking my wounds" and much forgiveness, I continued on.

That short chapter in my life ended and in 1983 I was back in Dallas working downtown for a private law firm as a legal assistant. It was one of those jobs that you get through a friend of a friend. I was in-between jobs and agreed to help out a lawyer in my friend's law firm until he could find someone for permanent hire. I could type and learned quickly how to file pleadings, research case law, type briefs, etc. It turned out that I was pretty good at it and enjoyed the people I was working with. Downtown Dallas in the 1980's was a fun place to work. I did not know it at the time, but this would become my livelihood for the next twenty-eight years. I was fortunate in my career to work for some kind and talented people.

In 1984 I was living as I recall, from paycheck to paycheck and struggling as a single woman in her later twenties in a teeny-weeny apartment with my cat. That was my life and I was happy. Then another unpredictable event happened that again sent my life in a new direction. This one came from my mother.

Chapter 4

The Letter

My mother's dear friend, Peggy Ladenberger, is a psychologist in Dallas, Texas. Peggy asked my mother on one occasion in the 1980s if she had ever given her adopted children permission to search for their birth parents. Peggy knew of my family's history. My mother told her "no, she had not," and that to her knowledge, none of her adopted children had ever shown any interest in searching. Peggy told Mom that in her experience, every adopted person she had ever counseled had been curious, on some level, but many were reluctant to follow through for fear of hurting the adoptive parents. My mother thought a lot about that conversation with Peggy and came to the conclusion that if she were to find out that she herself had been an adopted child, that she would certainly want to know the circumstances and history of her lineage.

The result of this conversation prompted my mother to write a letter to each of the adopted children in my family. The three adopted children received this letter from my mother on May 8, 1984. The very special letter we received on Mother's Day of that year was entitled "A Mother's Day Gift." The following letter is the catalyst that inspired and empowered me in so many ways and it was on that day that I made my decision to search for my biological parents. I am in awe of my mother's strength and sense of self. I am now a mother and have often asked myself if faced with this same circumstance, would I be able to write such a selfless letter. This is an exact duplication of the letter:

> May 8, 1984
>
> Dearest Barry, Beverly, and Brian,
>
> This is my Mothers' Day gift to you three. Our permission, though you have never needed it, for you to search for your roots. Please know that we love you and consider ourselves your parents. But I do know that, were I in your shoes, I would want

The Letter

to know from whence I came. And I have read so much lately that adoptive children are reticent about asking or searching for fear of hurting their adoptive parents. Such is not the case at all. I, too, would like to know them, and I encourage you.

Please don't be too judgmental of your natural mother. You were born before birth control pills, before abortion was legalized, and long before the "new" morality. Children raised by single mothers in those days were almost ostracized by society. So whatever she is like, bear in mind that she did what she felt was best for you at the time.

We wanted children to love and care for and couldn't have them. The fact that we later had two certainly doesn't change our feelings for you three. We were optimistic and immature enough to think we could help you all to develop into fine and wonderful adults—and that is exactly what you are, although you might not realize it yet. Also, in those days, environment was considered the most important factor in a child's development. Now, we think it is heredity. At any rate, we did not care to know anything about your parentage. Now, knowing each of you like I do, I think it would be so interesting to know your natural parents and the part your heredity has played in making you who you are!

I am enclosing some articles and the names of some organizations my dear psychologist friend recommended to me. I want you to read the articles before you do anything. You must be prepared for rejection, because that is what you might find. And I think some of these organizations might counsel with you on that. You just might find acceptance—you never know.

Just know that regardless of what you find, you have not lost anything! We are still here. And we are the ones who raised you and have loved you since the day we laid eyes on you. We will still love you.

As always,
MOM

She hand-wrote the following at the bottom of the page:

Bev, a new law was passed January 1984. You can write requesting records be opened.

Coincidental Pursuit

> Texas Dept. of Human Resources
> Special Services Div.
> Austin, TX 78769

Attn: Joyce Selms

> Search Line of Texas
> P.O. Box 157126
> Irving, Texas 75-15

    At the time my mother wrote the letter, I was happy and content with my life as a single woman in her late twenties trying to make her way in the world. Don't get me wrong, but the letter from my mother had inspired me! It was like being given a key to unlock something that, until that moment, I did not know how badly I had wanted. I could almost taste it! Why spoil such an ideal family situation, right? On the other hand, why not seek as much information as I could to satisfy not only my curiosity, but for health information, genetic predispositions, and so forth, for not only me, but my future children as well. I felt electrified! I was overwhelmed with a feeling of calm that was hard to explain, I was so at peace with the decision; and simultaneously felt a growing desire from within that I had never experienced before. I suddenly possessed such a passion to do this and I liked the way it made me feel. I was compelled and so driven to know the truth, to know my story. I was going to do this. Let the search begin.

Chapter 5
Searching for Stacia

I quickly became very aware of the huge learning curve when bringing up in conversation my plan to search for my birth parents. I found early on that not everyone shared the enthusiasm that I did. Some people I spoke with felt I was being ungrateful and believed that searching for my biological parents was a cruel and selfish act. One individual even expressed it as being the ultimate betrayal by a child. I was mortified at that assumption.

I learned to "tread lightly" and assess a situation before speaking too freely about my plan. I had to learn to get a feel for the way people viewed the topic of adoption and adoption searches before discussing my project in any detail. Some negative comments I took to heart and the negativity would stall my search, temporarily making me wonder and question whether or not I was doing the right thing. I would think about it and ultimately discuss it again with Mom and Dad, each time repeatedly returning to my quest with more determination than before. Bottom line, I did want to know where I came from and why I was given away! I needed my identity to be black and white. No more gray areas. I wanted to know my DNA makeup—to know as my mother so eloquently had put it in her letter to us, "from whence I came." Who was I, really? Were my bad habits inherited or learned? Where did my character traits—the good, the bad, and the ugly—really come from? Oh, and why was I so bad at math?

I had always wondered who "she," meaning my birth mother, might be. Someone famous? What had happened? Where did that funny bend in my elbows and those eyebrows come from—did she have those? I so badly wanted to see my reflection in somebody.

As a child I would pick up on certain things adults would say that were hard for me to process. I remember being out with my Dad and people stopping to tell me how much I looked like him. I'm sure they were just trying to be nice, but some of them knew I was adopted and it made me question their motivation. It made me feel like they thought I was stupid. I think now that those people were probably uncomfortable with adoption and looking back I feel certain they did not know they were confusing me and it hurt.

Growing up, I had always been mesmerized by the big families we knew with lots of children and where the siblings shared a likeness. I was determined to get a piece of that. Genetics became so interesting to me. I learned all the obvious genetic traits: can someone curl their tongue, are the earlobes attached or unattached. It always came back to the same question: Who was I, really? The letter gave me a freedom that I did not know I had been longing for, the okay to search. But where was I to begin?

In 1985 I began my search by writing to all of the organizations that were attached to the letter my mother had given me. I put my name and birth information on every "list" available at the time that would be compared to another "list" of parents looking for the children they had adopted out. Mind you, this was 1985 to 1986 and the Internet was not what it is today. Google and Ancestry.com, were not even "born,"—no pun intended—yet. I was contacted by one of the organizations and vividly remember a man coming to my apartment to talk to me about this "slippery slope," as he called it, about searching for birth parents. I recall that he was not very optimistic and seemed to be discouraging me. He was certainly not the inspiration I was hoping for.

Once again I got busy and life got in the way. Over the next months I received not one response from any of the many letters to this or that agency that I had posted to. I lost interest in the search for a while. This would become a kind of pattern:

- excitement
- new search idea
- more correspondence
- new lead
- dead end
- back to daily life

My next move to was contact the attorney who had handled the private adoption. Mom and Dad provided me with his name and I did contact him. I was told that the adoption records were only kept for ten years and that all of his records pertaining to this adoption had been destroyed. I do not think that is the law; I think that this was his personal policy. He was neither receptive nor supportive. I remember feeling like a scolded child when he asked me, "Do your parents know you are doing this?" I thought, really? I was devastated that so many clues had been destroyed.

When I look back through my box of "research"—I kept all of the correspondence, calendar pages noting this or that progress, napkins with scribbles on them with an idea, a matchbook with a new name or phone number—I am amazed that I persevered and did not get discouraged. It makes me very proud of myself for not giving up.

My parents had always told me that they knew very little about my birth mother. The story goes that in 1956 my father was a general practitioner at a medical clinic in East Dallas along with several other physicians. My father said he remembered one of his partners, Dr. James Goodson, (an OB/GYN), calling him into his office one day and telling him about a woman in the next room who had found herself "in a bad situation," meaning unmarried and pregnant. The woman had gotten off the bus outside the clinic and was sitting in his office. She wanted to put her baby up for adoption. This colleague knew that Ben and Betty were looking to adopt another child, so he had my dad look in. He told me later that he thought, "Well, I guess she looks all right," and decided right then and there that he and my mother would adopt her baby.

That baby turned out to be me. Lucky coincidence? Or was it a fateful and oh-so-fortunate bus stop? I will be the first one to tell you that whatever you want to call it, I call it the most fortunate day of my soon-to-be life outside the womb. My parents hired an attorney to arrange the paperwork for a private legal adoption which was the way it was handled in 1956, and then everyone waited for me to be born.

I asked my mom not too long ago to tell me about the day she picked me up. She had to stop and think and then said, "Well, we drove to the hospital and they handed you to me and I loved you from that moment." I also learned from her that day that there was a six-month time period wherein the birthmother could change her mind. Mom told me that she would often see women stopping to look at me at the grocery store, or while she was out running errands and it would make her wonder if that could be the woman that had given birth to me—had my birthmother changed her mind? I had not previously been aware of that fact.

I was amazed by the story. What a fortunate baby I was! Thank goodness my biological mother got off at that particular bus stop and thank goodness my dad was at work that day.

The next logical search idea was to contact my father's colleague, Dr. James Goodson, as he was the doctor that had the initial contact with my birth mother. Dr. Goodson had also overseen the prenatal care of my birth mother and performed the delivery. He was a sweet and dear family friend. I wrote to him on September 8, 1987, asking for any information he could remember or provide me with that would aid in my search. He did his due diligence and searched the hospital records to no avail. Dr. Goodson told me that he just couldn't remember her name but assured me that he would keep trying.

Bless his heart; little did I know how hard he in fact did work for me. On October 23, 1987, I received a telephone call from Dr. Goodson. He said, "Beverly, I have her name." My mother's name was Stacia Coryell! She was born in 1932. I was thrilled and of course curious. Had he remembered? He explained that being at his wit's end, he had placed a call to my dad and it was my dad who remembered her name, which in turn enabled Dr. Goodson to furnish me with a few records from the hospital. It was huge! I had a name and a birthday—oh, and I knew she was Catholic. My biological mother being of the Catholic faith was not an issue to me, it was just another tidbit of information that I had about her. That was about the extent of the information someone needed to be admitted to the hospital in 1956. The doctor was then able to find for me the records he had kept during her pregnancy. It turns out that my birth mother took a form of amphetamine during her pregnancy (which I have learned was not uncommon) to keep her from gaining too much weight.

A feeling washed over me—it was happening! And a question haunted me—where was she?

Chapter 6

The Stall

    I immediately hit a roadblock in locating Stacia Coryell born in 1932. I had just enough information, but not enough. I began thinking that this could be all that I would ever know. But again, the proverbial carrot had been dangled and motivated me to continue to ask questions and listen for clues to anything and anyone that might give me a leg up. I desperately needed "a someone" that might "know someone." I was just at the beginning of the many valuable lessons I would learn along the way -- one being what a small world it really is if you ask the right questions to the right people at the right time. That was a very important skill I learned and honed throughout my search.

    I was fortunate enough to have one of the attorneys at the law firm I worked in downtown learn of my search. He told me that he had an acquaintance in Wisconsin who had aided people in searches such as mine and that she had told him some fascinating search stories. He insisted that I speak with her and kindly gave me her contact information. I wrote my first letter to Ms. Mary Sue Wedl on November 7, 1987. I shared with her any and all information I had and also told her that my father seemed to recall that my birth mother was a registered nurse, perhaps in the Chicago area. I so appreciated Ms. Wedl, not only for all of the legwork in the Chicago area she did for me, but also that she was able to furnish me with the names and addresses of the State of Illinois Department of Education and Registration to request names of nurses in Illinois. Obtaining this information was huge back then. There was no Internet or Google search engines to find the addresses and other information that I needed. She also coached me on library research, the ins and outs of how to read tax rolls, how to check the marriage and death certificates, and what dates to use going forward and backward to cover my time frame. It was a tiresome and time-consuming task.

I visited the Herschel Street address in Dallas I had acquired from the hospital record received from Dr. Goodson. It was the address listed on the hospital record as Stacia's place of residence in 1956. I knocked on the door but the occupant knew nothing of Stacia. It was rental property so many people had come and gone from this property over the many years. It was a frightening thing for me to do, but I did not trust anyone else to do it, and I wanted to see the neighborhood with my own eyes. I wanted to see what she had seen while pregnant with me. . I walked the street and knocked on doors up and down the street looking for someone, maybe someone older who had been in the neighborhood for many years, that might remember her. I struck out. I remember asking myself, "Can I do this?" The answer was always "Yes, just use your head and come at this from a different angle."

On December 17, 1987, I received a letter from the State of Illinois saying there was no one by the name of Stacia Coryell working in the state. I was so disappointed. I quit working on the search for a while. How had I come this far, only to be stone-walled again? There had to be a way to find this person who was my biological mother. The best information I would get and that eventually would lead me to her came from a most unexpected place.

Chapter 7
The Nail Salon

*"...what you learn today, for no reason
at all, will help you discover all the wonderful
secrets of tomorrow."*
-- Norton Juster

I wish I could remember who was giving the party, but I don't.

What I do remember is splurging and deciding to have my nails done for the party. It was the late 1980s and fingernails were long and manicures on the pricey side. Certainly a "once in a while" treat. I decided to have my nails done on Friday before the weekend of the party while on my lunch hour downtown. I had never been to this particular salon before but had been referred by a friend.

The appointment was uneventful as far as a nail appointment goes. I sat there for about forty-five minutes and just chatted, making small talk, but something about the nail technician's questions and chatting led me to tell her "my story" of the ongoing and stalemated search for my birth mother. As I mentioned earlier, I didn't do this very often—but something about the pertinent questions she was asking had me going full force. She seemed genuinely interested. When I left she called out to me, "Hey, wait a minute, can I get your phone number?" This was a little out of the ordinary but I assumed she wanted my number to solicit future business from me. I just jotted down my work number, paid her for her service, and left. I returned to work and struggled to use the keyboard in a truly efficient manner due to those long, but oh-so-pretty, fingernails.

About an hour after returning to work my desk phone rang. I answered my usual law firm greeting and the woman on the other end of the phone conversation was the nail technician I had just visited. I will, for lack of memory, call her Susan. I was totally dumbfounded with what she said to me during the conversation. Susan told me that her best friend had also been involved in a search for her biological parents. This friend of Susan's had some health issues and badly needed genetic family health-related information. The friend had not been successful for a long time, but then found her biological father who, unbeknownst to her, had lived around the corner from her for years. Unfortunately, her information came too late as he had passed away shortly before she found him. Susan said it was very hard on her friend and that after our chat during my nail appointment she had placed a call to her friend and relayed to her my to date search efforts. Susan's friend, who shall remain nameless because I was never given her name, was moved by my efforts and told Susan that she had the ability to, and wanted to, give me a one-time gift—but it came with some conditions.

Ms. Nameless was currently working for an unknown government agency and, although it was not allowed, she had access to and could possibly furnish me with some information I badly needed. Information was what it would take to piece my puzzle together. She did not want me to "lose any more time" as in any search for birth parents, time is not on your side. Susan told me that she had already given Ms. Nameless my phone number and that I should make myself available, as she would be calling me shortly.

As for the conditions, this is how it had to work: She would call and I was to give, as quickly as possible, all of the information I had on Stacia Coryell. The telephone on her end would do a series of clicks every thirteen seconds as she would be switching between phone lines so as not to be traced. She could not leave a trail. Our conversation must not be traceable. It would be as if it never happened. I could hardly breathe—of course, I agreed to these conditions! Ms. Nameless was jeopardizing her career to help a complete stranger. I was not to converse with her—information only. Then and only IF she was able to gather any information, she would call back and the same protocol was to be followed. No conversation. She told me simply to "be ready to write fast." It was over that quickly—and click, the phone line went dead. I sat for the longest time with the telephone receiver in my hand, just staring. It seemed so crazy. I soon recovered and I remember blurting out a kind of giggle and thought, yeah, right, and went back to work. The whole scenario was just too weird. Was this a joke?

About thirty minutes later the phone rang again. It was Ms. Nameless! My hands, pretty nails and all, were shaking. She asked, "Are you ready?" and she began speaking to me in a slow but deliberate, monotone voice. Suddenly I had my birthmother's full first, middle, and last name, maiden name, a Social Security number, birthdate, marriage date, an address, a previous address, place of employment, yearly income, and the telephone number of my birth mother—but most surprisingly of all, I had the name of yet another brother, Cameron, who I learned later went by Cam. That made five brothers! She was right, the information came fast and the clicks and static on the line made it difficult to understand. The phone line would seem to go completely dead, and then she would be back speaking in the same deliberate monotone voice. She would repeat nothing and at the end she simply said, "This is my gift to you, use this information wisely. I wish you luck and hope this helps in your endeavor. Please be careful how you use it and be prepared to be unprepared for whatever you might find. Keep in mind this will not be easy. Good luck to you." She continued, "I will never have contact with you again and will destroy your phone number and all records on my end when we disconnect. Good luck and good bye."

Looking back on that day, I am sure that I was in total shock. After the call concluded, I remember just sitting at my work desk holding the phone receiver, staring into it and thinking, "I did it!" Could it have been that easy, a phone call? Again the theme of right place, right time wiggled through my brain. I couldn't believe what had just happened. I volleyed back and forth, being excited, to scared, back to being excited. I had found her, it was no longer my "job" to search—yes, I had done it! One simple phone conversation with a complete stranger had just given me the key to unlock so many doors from my past. It was so exciting! I remember that I could not stop smiling, my cheeks hurt. I was in total disbelief. I had just found out who and where the person was that gave birth to me.

If the expression "be careful what you ask for" was ever apropos, this was surely that time in my life. Now I knew she lived in Houston. Okay. Good. But how and when do I make contact with her? I needed some time to think that part through. I, of course, called my mom and dad next and told them my news. They were as dumbfounded as I still was. I decided my next move was to call my great friend who lived in Houston, Richard Davies. Richard and I met in college and I have dearly loved him for years. We had kept up with each other since college, and I don't know why, but I thought I wanted him to drive by the address I had been given for Stacia's house and report back to me what he saw. He was certainly closer physically than I was to Stacia. It had to be done that way because that was long before everyone carried cell phones. I called and he said that he would be happy to accommodate. He asked for the address and when I recited it to him, he just started laughing. I will never forget feeling so puzzled and agitated with him. His response was, "Oh my God, are you kidding me?" Well, no, I was not "kidding him" and I was slow at seeing the humor. When he recovered he explained that he knew exactly where the house was. It was located just down the street from his grandmother's house (the house he has since purchased and where he currently lives). Richard said he could throw a rock from there and hit it. I was dumbfounded and felt like objects were being hurled at me from another galaxy. How could this happen – how could it be that Richard knew where the house was in a town the size of Houston? What a coincidence, right?

Richard took to my task and returned my call after his reconnaissance mission. He gave me a very detailed blow-by-blow description of the house, its condition, cars in the driveway, and so forth. Richard said that he had seen a young man in the front yard—a tall, good-looking guy with long blond hair. Richard said he assumed that must be my half-brother, Cam, and Richard said he remembers thinking to himself, "Man, if you people only knew what I know!" So there I was, the woman who was always hungry for information suddenly finding herself on extreme information overload. I needed to breathe!

That weekend I began calling the phone number for Stacia that I had been given in the clandestine phone call from Ms. Nameless. It was my holy grail! The first couple of times I dialed the phone number there was no answer, but on my third attempt a woman picked up the receiver . . . and I froze. My heart was pounding in my chest. I hung up. On the evening that I placed this call I had invited some good friends over for moral support, I suppose. They were each very encouraging in their own special ways and were my security blanket.

After slamming down my receiver, I remember one of them saying, "Bev, what are you so afraid of, she can't eat you—just do it." The statement made sense. I waited for one hour, to the minute. I mustered the courage and made the call. This was it—and this time she answered. The words I said to her seemed to stick in my throat like cotton. I told her who I was and why I had reason to believe that she was my mother. I spat forth names, dates, and locations—I rapidly threw at her everything I had in my arsenal of information that I had spent years gathering – my ammunition so to speak. I did not let her speak at all. I simply had to make her understand that I was not a threat. This was my one shot. The words, once they begin to come out of my mouth flowed through that phone line like dialogue from a well-written script. I simply knew in my heart at that moment that I was saying all of the right things. It is hard to explain, but I knew I had gotten it right.

I do not know exactly what I expected her voice to sound like that on that day, but her voice was not like I thought it would sound in my ears. She was very short with me when I had finally paused long enough in my "sales pitch" for her to speak. She gave very clipped answers that made my spine tingle and I fought down the feeling of dread I felt bubbling up inside. I found her to be not at all receptive and I remember feeling sort of like a pinpricked balloon that was slowly, but steadily, losing its air. During that initial phone call Stacia repeatedly denied being my mother. However, towards the end of our conversation there was something about the way she asked me when my birthday was. When I told her my date of birth, there was an audible intake of breath and a hesitation I heard through the receiver. I knew that I had found her.

I hung up the receiver. The conversation left me feeling very off center, as if the world had shifted a little off its axis. I was physically light headed. The feeling was one I had never experienced and very strange. There were so many questions I needed and wanted answers to. I was dangling on the edge of the cliff. Would I fall off and fail after coming this far? I needed a way to regain my balance, but how?

I left everything alone for one week to give each of us time to think. It was exhausting. I was trying to come to terms in my head why she was not as excited as I was about all of this. I regained my balance by attempting to feel what she must be feeling. I had been at this for a long time and she had been caught totally off-guard. She had no "heads-up" warning whatsoever and had not been prepared for me to reenter her life. I knew it was only fair that I respect that and give her time to decide how she wanted to deal with our situation. Once again in my life, I had to learn to swallow the "patience pill," and it was not going down easily.

It was a long and excruciating week spent trying not to think things to death. I replayed our conversation over and over in my head. I did not talk to many people about what had recently transpired as it felt way too personal—and I was so scared. What if she did not like me, or worse yet, what if she did not care at all. I felt physically ill and I began to wonder if I really was prepared for any scenario.

One week later to the day I dialed Stacia's number again. I truly did not know what to expect from my second attempt to contact her. I had tried to fully prepare myself for her to just hang up on me when she heard my voice.

It was before the days of caller ID on telephones, so she would not know before answering where the call originated. I have thought about this a lot and although caller ID may sound like a little thing, had my phone call come to her with the caller ID information showing my name as the caller, she might have glanced at the number, recognized it was me, and chosen not to answer. It would have made it easier and less personal for her that way. This line of thinking brought me to the conclusion that as much as technology, or more the lack of technology, in the mid-1980s hindered my search—expensive long distance, no cell phones and no Internet—this same lack of technology was probably what allowed my call that day to be received by Stacia.

It was during this second phone call, right away, that Stacia acknowledged herself as my birth mother. She has never said so, but I suppose she realized that I was not going away. This was huge! I was so excited. She had just told me that, yes, she was my mother! We chatted and I remember feeling very awkward. I had a million questions but they just wouldn't come out on the phone.

Deep down, I knew exactly what the problem was, why I was feeling so awkward—I needed to see her in person. Stacia wanted me to know that there was just one other person that knew about her pregnancy with me, a good friend who had moved with her here from out of state and had been with her the entire time. Other than that, no one else knew anything about my birth. These "no ones" included the father and my half-brother from her later marriage. I understood what she was telling me and I agreed to her terms. My half-brother would not find about me from me. My reassurance to keep her secret was paramount. I totally understood her fears and told her so. I would not reveal a secret that had been kept at that time for thirty-two years.

Bowden family 1972
From top left:
Barry, Ben
Betty, Beverly
Blake, Brad, Brian

Ben & Betty
1948

Ben and Betty on a cruise.

Ben & Betty Wedding
1948

Mom & Dad
Ben & Betty Bowden
2006

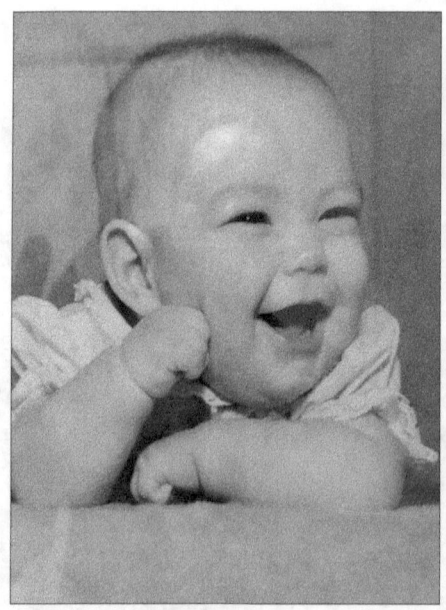

McKinley
Four Months Old

McKinley - Chi Omega
2012

Bev & McKinley - 2010

Bev & McKinley - 2007

Bowden Family Christmas - 2012

Mike and Bev Wedding - 1995

My four brothers - from left - Blake, Barry, Bev, Brian and Brad

Mike, Wes and Casey

McKinley and Wes

Betty Bowden - 2013

McKinley with Jackson - 2014

Chapter 8

The Reunion

In October 1988, after several more covert phone conversations, Stacia agreed to meet me in person. She was as hesitant about our meeting as I was insistent. I had to be careful when calling her for her son lived with her and this was all a secret, remember? We agreed that I would fly to Houston and take her to lunch. Stacia wanted to meet me at an Olive Garden. Okay, the date was set—I was going to meet my biological mother! I truly went out of my comfort zone on this one and, silly me, went to a hair salon and got what I now call the worst "perm" of my life. I do not know what I was thinking. I remember thinking, "Oh no, this is not how it was supposed to be." In my dreams our first meeting was perfect, but apparently this first meeting was destined to be just as strange as my hair was badly permed.

I called Richard and he picked me up at the airport. I will never forget his face when he saw me—the reaction was to my hair, He was nice but I could tell it was as bad as I knew it was. I had waited thirty-two years to meet my birth mother, and this was not the way I had pictured it, but it was really happening. Richard and I had a little time to kill before I was to meet Stacia at the restaurant so Richard took me by his mother's house and I remember her offering me a drink. I remember her saying, "If an occasion ever warranted a drink, I think this one surely qualifies." Bless her heart. I was a nervous wreck. The plan was that Richard would drop me off at the restaurant and when Stacia and I were finished I would call him and he would come pick me up.

I entered the restaurant. Just another Olive Garden, but this one felt different. I felt electrified. The delicious smells, the noise of all the voices were a blur, all so familiar but at the same time so foreign. I stood at the oversized wooden front door with the "Please Come In" sign. "Just open it!" I kept telling myself. "Through that door is the person you have been waiting your whole life to meet—the woman you have spent so much time and effort to find.'" Then I saw her. Our eyes met and we held each other's gaze. There she was! I was breathing so fast it is amazing that I did not hyperventilate. We gave a quick hug and once over of each other. I could not quit staring at her. I was not feeling what I thought that I might. No tears of joy, no animosity—she was just a woman.

    Stacia was taller than I had imagined with auburn hair and freckles. That is the polar opposite of me, although I am on the tall side. We sat and made small talk. We waived the poor waitress off several times, explaining that we wanted to visit for a bit before ordering our lunch. Stacia was thoughtful and had brought a few pictures of her son and deceased husband. She told me about her life in Houston, in no great detail, just a little about home and work. I felt her to be very guarded in the information she was sharing with me, but I was fine with that. It was a start. Most of my questions were answered in a very forthright, but abstract manner. It is hard to explain, it was as if she were just skimming the top. There was no depth or substance to the information about her family, her history, or the sequence of events that I was craving. My searching skills had me programmed to find facts, boom, boom, write them down, make a list, and then on to the next lead. The information she was telling me was just not coming fast enough. I was terribly impatient. Getting direct answers from her in this dialogue was like pulling teeth. Again, I was navigating in unchartered territory. I have yet to find a step-by-step guide entitled Protocol of How to Meet Your Birthmother anywhere.

    Coincidently, my father had remembered correctly. She was a nurse by vocation. She had moved to Houston after my birth and gone to work nursing. During this

Stacia – Age 32
The picture she handed me the day we met.

The Reunion

lunch, Stacia cautioned me about drinking red wine, saying that she could not tolerate it probably because of the percentage of American Indian blood passed to her, and that was probably the reason I was here. I wish I had known that earlier; it explained a lot. Stacia's mother was full blood Sioux Indian.

We carried on and had a lovely lunch, but I could not tell you to this day what was on the plate in front of me. The fork was traveling from the plate to my mouth purely out of muscle memory. I was studying her every move, gesture, her mannerisms and her manners.

We visited easily back and forth. However, the big grey elephant was still in the room. Who was my father? This was the question I wanted to ask. Stacia had said early on in our conversation that "he" did not know about her pregnancy. This left me wondering if she had just abruptly left Nebraska with her secret. She certainly had to know that I was anxious to know the whole story and that I wanted more than anything for her to get around to talking about the subject. I was starving for information and she was feeding it to me one crumb of at a time.

I studied this woman from her pinky fingers to her pinky toes. Skin tone, eyebrow shape, I was looking for that funny bend in the elbows. As I mentioned earlier, I was so keenly aware and was committing to memory the littlest nuances, posture, hand gestures. I was like a sponge trying to soak up everything about her in the time span of a lunch. Yes, I even asked her to take off her shoes so I could see if maybe our feet had any resemblance. No resemblance at all. There was nothing. I felt at such a loss.

Stacia realized what I was doing, of course, and just shook her head and said, "Bev, you look just like him." She answered many of my questions regarding health history and where she came from, but the one question she would not answer was, "Well, if I look just like him, who is 'him'"?

Then Stacia next made a bold statement to me. She leaned back in her chair and made direct eye contact..

"Well, since you have proven yourself to be such a good detective, then perhaps you might be as lucky in finding your father," she said. "The only information I will give you is that his first name is Bruce and that he had been a gifted football player and had played the sport at Hastings College, Nebraska."

That was it! I wonder if she had pre-planned that or if it just came to her. I never thought to ask. I was stunned. It even crossed my mind that maybe she didn't remember his last name. No way, I pushed that thought completely out of my head.

Stacia made it clear and wanted me to understand that Bruce would not remember her and certainly did not know about me. She reiterated that he had been very popular and that if I were to find him, that he would not remember her. What? That statement haunted me. I remember looking into her eyes after she made it not knowing what I was seeing. Looking into Bruce's eyes would prove to be completely different.

Giving birth to me had changed and completely rearranged her life and I couldn't help but feel that she would like to keep the past in the past. That was, however, not what I was feeling at all. I was just warming up and I was on a mission. Ready, set, go!

Stacia suddenly changed the subject by asking me if I liked my name. "Excuse me?" I was taken aback. "Yes, I like my name. Why?"

She began telling me that was not what she had named me. Stacia's chosen name for me was Rebecca. This statement came completely out of left field; it had never even occurred to me that I had been given another name. My mouth fell open and I remember feeling dizzy and staring at the white plate in front of me. I was overcome by such a strange sensation of falling for a moment, like the floor was suddenly gone, but I regained my composure. I remember giggling out of nervousness and the commercial slogan "Never let them see you sweat" came into my mind. Really? I did not want to her to see that she had thrown me a curve ball, and I wasn't ready for the pitch. I would never let that happen again.

We finished our lunch and I was going to call Richard to come and get me when Stacia said that she wouldn't mind giving me a ride back to Richard's house. Nice, I thought. We walked together to the parking lot and got into her old, light blue LTD. As we drove off she said, "Oh, I need to make one stop, do you mind?" We pulled into a Kmart store so she could buy a mop. Oh my, I found myself just laughing out loud. I had waited thirty-two years to meet this woman and on our first meeting we stop at Kmart to buy a mop. We also stopped by her home and that also surprised me. I took a few pictures of her in the yard with an expensive camera I had borrowed from my parents. She asked me to follow her into the house and said to "just follow her lead." I was shocked, but I followed in every sense of the word. The house was just a normal house, with a porch, a front door, and everything else I saw as normal and as to be expected. But through my eyes I was seeing, for the first time, a porch and a front door that could have been, through different circumstances, where I would have grown up. My knees felt weak. I was trying to take everything in while posing as an impostor. Nothing, and I mean nothing, was real at that moment!

We entered the house and there stood my half-brother, Cam, with no shirt on. He was as tall as Richard had told me he was and very handsome. She quickly introduced me as the daughter of a co-worker who was in town. I remember thinking, "Oh, that's who I am today?" Cam politely shook my hand and I am sure he thought me quite strange because I wanted to see if the palms of his hands were as rough as mine have always been so I held his hand a little longer than I probably should have. Thank goodness he seemed not to notice. I thought he treated her a bit gruff, mumbling something about dinner, and then just walking off. She didn't seem to take notice or offense.

Stacia - Year Unknown

Stacia reached up and removed a five-inch-by-seven-inch portrait of herself from the wall. She handed it to me and told me that the picture was taken when she was thirty-two, the same age as I was then. I accepted the picture and she then drove me down the street back to Richard's house. Before I got out of her car, she reached over and felt the palm of my hands, apparently she knew what I was doing when shaking Cam's hand. She simply said, "My mother had those rough hands, they were just like yours." That was it. I got out of the car and we said "goodbye." There was no promise of "call you next week" or "see you soon." It just wasn't like that. Not a bad feeling, but not a warm and fuzzy vibe, either.

I was a mess when I saw Richard after meeting Stacia. I had so much to tell him. I felt good . . . and bad . . . and overall kind of strange. I needed to process all that had transpired. We talked and talked. Richard had arranged for us to go to a comedy club that night and we happened to see the incredibly funny comedian Jeff Foxworthy. It was before he became so popular with his comedic bit on how stupid we all are at times. "You might be a redneck if . . . " It was so refreshing. We all laughed until we cried. I am so grateful for the distraction after the sensory overload of the day. It was truly just what the doctor ordered. Thank you again, Richard.

I flew back to Dallas the next day and had a date for a party that night. I was excited and in a hurry to get ready, I had so much to tell everyone. I also wanted to get the film developed in the borrowed camera. I was in my bathroom and pulled the camera out of my bag so as to not hurt it and I swear, I could not have thrown it with any better accuracy straight into the toilet. I literally screamed "Nooooooooo!" Not at all sure what to do next, I grabbed the camera and called a Wolf Camera store and probably sounded like a crazy woman telling them what I had done to my camera. I explained that the film contained once- in-a-lifetime pictures and I had to save them. This is the strange part. They advised me to fill a gallon Baggie with toilet water and put the camera back in it and bring it to them. They explained that you don't want the film to dry out, leaving a residue on the film. I did as instructed and I am sure to this day they thought I was indeed crazy. I certainly got some looks carrying a Baggie full of toilet water with a camera in it into the store. They worked and worked and were able to save me only two pictures, but my parents' camera was ruined beyond repair. I felt so stupid.

I replayed my lunch with Stacia over and over in my head. I had questions: Had it gone well? Did she like me? I had to stop. I was back in my routine and things were okay, but my curiosity was just not going to leave me alone. I was obsessed with finding this man. I would play one scenario after another, like an old movie, in my head. It was like an itch I could not scratch and no matter how much I distracted myself I knew I was not going to be okay until I found Bruce. I kept thinking, how dare she do this – how callous it was to give me so little information and then challenge me.

Game on!

Chapter 9

The Search for My Father

I needed a forward direction. The captain of my search ship needed to step up her game, so that is what I did. I came up with a plan, a long shot of a plan that was just a little on the shady side, but it was still a plan. The only facts that I knew for certain were that my birth father played football for Hastings College in Hastings, Nebraska; his name was Bruce; and that I looked like him.

Hmm, I needed pictures of him. But how?

I needed a subterfuge. I had to find some way to obtain a visual of college athletes at Hastings College from the 1950s. So I composed a letter to "anyone" in the Archives Department at Hastings College in Nebraska who could assist me with my thesis research. In my letter, I presented myself as a graduate student doing a study on football players between the years 1953 and 1958 (I was born in 1956, so I thought that would be broad enough) named Bruce. I put a bunch of catch phrases and research type criteria in my correspondence, but my main concern and point I was trying to convey was that I needed them to forward me pictures. I really did not think that this hair-brained scheme was going to work, but I was desperate and certainly willing to try. And, as they say, "stranger things have happened." They certainly did for me.

On January 25, 1989, I received my reply from Hastings College in the form of a thick, standard-sized envelope that arrived at my office addressed to me with the return address "Hastings College Alumni Association." My heart stopped! I stared at the envelope that could possibly change my life and turned it over and over in my hands. I remember running my fingers along the taped seal and studying the postmark. I still have that envelope—call me sentimental or whatever you like. My plan had worked. Or had it? I was visibly shaking as I opened the envelope. The letter read as follows:

This is all we could release. Hope it satisfies your curiosity. Good luck.

> *HC Alumni Association*
> *Cathy Toms, Intern*

The packet contained a page full of faces from the school yearbook. My eyes landed immediately on a circled picture at the bottom of the page of an incredibly handsome young man; it read Bruce Edwards, Hastings. I was able to pick him out of the team picture immediately. He wore the number 20 on his jersey. I stood and stared, dumbstruck, at the picture of the man at the bottom of the page; I looked just like him! Also included were several poses of him in his football uniform and three articles written about him. He had been a star football player and the articles glorifying his football ability and game winning tactics. One covered the Hastings 26-19 win over Colorado State: "Early in the second quarter Borden covered a Colorado fumble on the Greeley four, and Edwards carried it over for his second touchdown of the game." Another article cited that "Edwards, who set an NCC scoring record of seventy-two points in 1954, finished second behind Peru's Del Stoltenberg, who had fifty. Bruce had sixty for the season, forty-five in conference play."

A close co-worker walked by my desk about that time and picked Bruce right off the page as my father. Oh, my, I had done it. I was holding in my hand the last puzzle piece. I had located him! A feeling of warmth, and pride for a man that did not even know I was alive washed over me like a wave.

Surprisingly, on January 30, 1989, I received another envelope from Hastings College, this one from the Communication Arts Department. Apparently, two separate people were working on my bogus request. This letter read as follows:

> *Sorry that I took so long to get these copies, but I think they are what you are looking for.*
> *Please let me know if we can be of any further help.*
>
> *Sincerely, Kathy _____*

This packet contained a different picture of the football team with Bruce's name circled and several articles about his football contributions to Hastings College and a bonus, a recent picture of him and his wife

The Search for My Fa

celebrating their silver wedding anniversary. I immediately noted their wedding date —November 10, 1956. A quick calculation, and I learned that I was seven months old when he married. Also included was a picture of Bruce receiving the Elk's Club award voting him Elk of the Year. Civic minded, too? Wow! This meant I had all the pieces to the puzzle. I knew what came next.

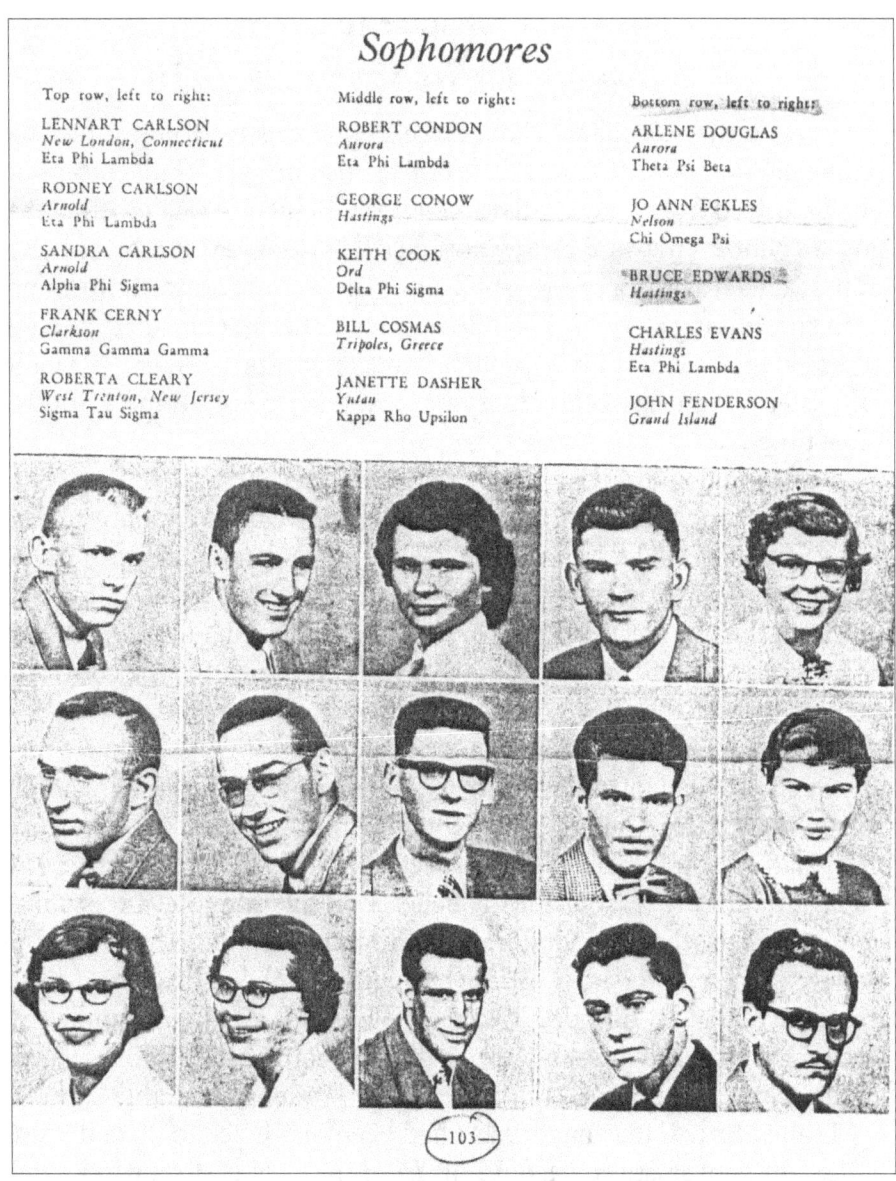

Yearbook photo copy I received with Bruce (bottom center).

Chapter 10
Making Contact . . . Again

I was quite reluctant to make the phone call to Bruce. I had the phone number but the sting of the not-so-distant unfavorable reception I had received from Stacia still burned fresh. Remembering too, that this guy was not even aware of my existence, left me wary and scared. The initial contact with Bruce would again play as a movie scenario in my head considering all of his possible reactions: the good, the bad, and the all-so-possible-and-entirely-probable total rejection scenario. I would call, listen to him say hello, then freeze, and hang up. I think I did this three times.

Realizing that I needed help, I told my father the trouble I was having. I guess looking back, I was putting up a brave front and more afraid of a rejection then I let on. My father asked me for Bruce's phone number and simply and very matter-of-factly said, "I know how to do this," and he dialed the number. I held my breath. I was amazed, touched, and any and every other off-the-chart emotion you can think of at the conversation I witnessed that day.

As my father dialed Bruce's number, my heart was pounding. Bruce answered and Dad introduced himself. He explained who he was and the reason for his call. Dad just started telling him my story. He explained that I had reason to believe that Bruce may be my biological father and then gave him the reasons for my belief. Dad told him that I was a nice young woman searching for her roots and wanted nothing from him but to have some answers and satisfy her curiosity about where she came from. He reassured him that I was not a nut case looking for money. It was such a kind and unselfish act on the part of my father, as one man to another. I will never forget that day and the kindness my father showed.

I called Bruce later that day as I had been instructed to do and it was a pleasant conversation. I liked him from the very first moment. I felt

Making Contact . . . Again

warmed just by talking to him as weird as that might sound, but a void had been filled, and I made it happen. Needless to say, there were many questions on both our parts—and, no, he did not remember Stacia. He explained that the 1950s were a crazy time for him. Bruce had gone to play professional football for the Canadian Tiger Cats right after college. He was then drafted to play for the Washington Redskins. As Bruce so aptly put it, he got around a bit. He was a good-looking young man making a lot of money and he liked to party.

During our first conversation, Bruce also told me that he was not totally surprised by my phone call. He had received a phone call and had been given a sort of "heads up" from the dean of Hastings College who happened to be a friend of his. The dean of the college had called Bruce to say that he thought that someone might be looking for him. Apparently word had gotten to the dean of my request for the thesis research pictures and the dean saw right through my ruse of posing as a graduate student. He had already called Bruce and said, "Buddy, somebody's looking for you, bet your past is about to catch up with you." Bruce was a good-hearted man who always saw the humor in a situation, so there was no harm done.

Bruce wanted to meet and I was excited. Our first meeting was a month later. He rode shotgun down from Nebraska to Texas in a friend's eighteen-wheeler and I was to meet them at a corporate apartment the trucking company kept off of Interstate Highway 635 and Preston Road. My parents went with me, as I still did not know much about this man. We all went to dinner and had a wonderful time. I stared at him and he stared at me. My mother said it was so cute. It was one of those moments you freeze in your mind. He had an easy going way about him and I could see why people liked him so much. I could not take my eyes off of him. When I looked into his eyes I felt the strangest sensation that I was looking into my own eyes. It was overwhelming and I loved it. We hugged and I could smell his cologne, we held hands and we stared. It was like nothing I had ever experienced in my life. My father in Dallas offered to pay for a DNA test if we weren't sure of our lineage, but he also added, "But from where I'm sitting, its obvious." We all laughed.

That was the beginning of a long and loving friendship. Bruce explained to me that he adopted a daughter in 1957 as he thought he could not have children. This daughter had recently searched for her own birth parents and did so without his blessing. I think there were some bad feelings as a result of this on both sides. He was not supportive and didn't make it easy for her. I think in hindsight he regretted how he had handled the situation with his adopted daughter, Pam. He later told me that it was a difficult and awkward conversation when he told her about me—something to do with "eating crow" is how he described his recollection to me. I eventually met Pam and her husband, Rick. We visited back and forth by telephone several times.

I believe it was November when the four of them traveled from Nebraska to visit me. It would be the first time I met Pam in person. The four of us, Pam and her husband and Bruce and his girlfriend, Alice, had flown in and we were picking them up for dinner. Alice Erickson was Bruce's longtime girlfriend and she is a wonderful person. She cared for Bruce as no one else could. She cared for him through his fight with cancer and proved to not only be my father's girlfriend, but became a good friend to me along the way. She was so accepting and opened her house to me on many occasions. Bruce was very lucky to have her in his life.

My father in Dallas hosted a fabulous dinner at the Celebration Restaurant on Lover's Lane. I will never forget what I wore to that dinner—a black sweater dress, black boots, and a black belt with silver conchos that Mom and Dad had brought me back from a trip they took to Utah. My parents purchased the belt at Robert Redford's ranch. We arrived to pick them up and Pam came out wearing the exact dress, boots, and belt. We both stood there dumbfounded—undeniably, another strange coincidence. I roared with laughter, for Pam was my sister through adoption, not blood, which made the whole occasion even stranger. It was so much fun and we had a wonderful time.

Bruce and I became very close and spoke by telephone at least once a week. We developed a strong and loving relationship. I learned that Bruce had an older brother who lived in California and that he had lost a younger sister, Beatrice, at age twenty-one to polio. He brought a picture of "Bea," as they called her. We shared an uncanny likeness. Pam said it took her breath away. Bruce and Pam also told me about his mother, Pansy. They both looked at me and asked if I had inherited her gift? When I asked what gift they were speaking of, they said in unison that "she was a psychic." In my mind I was thinking, "Well, that would explain some things, but then just really muddy up the water on others."

Making Contact . . . Again

So I replied that I had not received that special gift. They had wonderful stories about Pansy. She ran a kind of "out in the woods" boarding-type house and was known to have housed, fed, and entertained some well known and notorious politicians, outlaws, and other infamous individuals of the time when she was young. If those two were referring to her as "a real character," I can only imagine what Pansy must have been like. I was so touched when Bruce told me that his mother would have joyfully welcomed me into the family regardless of the circumstances. That felt good.

Bruce and I talked weekly through phone calls and made several visits back and forth. He had a keen wit, was a wonderful storyteller, and his delivery of a joke, which is becoming a lost art, was extraordinary. I am thankful for the thirteen years I did have with him.

Chapter 11
A Marriage, a Birth and a Death

I married again in 1991. My husband was Bill Risko. I met him through some friends at the Blue Goose Restaurant in Dallas. Bill went by the nickname of Cisco in the restaurant business. He was the general manager of this popular Mexican food establishment. We dated for one year before our marriage. Bill was divorced and shared custody of his daughter Lauren. We all got along great and she would spend every other weekend with us that first year. I became pregnant with McKinley in February of 1991 and we were all so happy and excited. I gave birth to our daughter, McKinley, in October 1992. I was so proud of her and she is my biggest accomplishment in life. She was and still is absolutely precious, and that would be the name my dad would call her, Precious, from the start. Shortly before McKinley's birth Bruce was flying out to California to see and visit with his older brother, Beryl. Bruce had a short layover at Dallas-Fort Worth International Airport and Bill and I were able to go and visit with him for a short time. Yes, Bruce was a nut. When we arrived at the bar where we were to meet him, Bruce was standing out in front holding court with whoever would stop and talk. He was hold- ing a sign that read, "Looking for my daughter." When people would ask, he would start telling them about our story of finding each other. It was so much fun and filled me with pride!

Shortly after McKinley was born, Bill had planned a trip with his assistant manager to Mexico to purchase new chairs for the restaurant dining room. Bill spoke some Spanish, but Jeff, the assistant manager, was fluent in the language. I knew they would be careful and anticipated no problem. The Dallas Cowboys had just won the Super Bowl and the big parade was planned the day they left. Bill called me several times on their way down south of the border using the giant cell phone of that era. The reception was not great but he was just checking in on all that was going on at home with the celebration. He had many friends who played for the team and was a great fan of the Dallas Cowboys. I heard from him that night when they arrived at the border town they were staying in before crossing over into Mexico the next day. He was complaining about the condition of the hotel on the border. Apparently, their accommodations were a bit sketchy. Bill told me he would call the next day. McKinley was four months old and she and I were just getting our routine of packing for daycare, driving to daycare, and driving myself to work down pat. I did not hear from him that day, February 10, 1993, but just chalked it up to him being busy securing the chairs.

I had a funny feeling the next day, an uneasy feeling. I now know that it was a premonition. My co-workers joked with me about my concern and said Bill probably met some Mexican senoritas—ha, ha. They were trying to distract me with humor. I did not hear from him that night either, and in my heart, I knew something was wrong.

The next day, February 11, 1993, was another day that changed my life forever. I was sitting at my desk in my office and suddenly looked up to see my father standing there. I knew instantly without him saying a word that something bad had happened. A feeling came over me and I asked, "He's dead, isn't he?" I will never forget the look on his face. My dad confirmed what I had said and took me home with him. Seeing Dad standing at my desk is an image that is burned into my memory. It is like a "freeze frame" in a movie even after all of these years. I rode home with my father and I left my car for one of the attorneys to drive to my parents' house. I had never seen my father cry before that day. I was in shock. Widowed with a new baby at thirty-six years of age, I felt I had fallen into a vast abyss.

We will never truly know what happened, but Bill, Jeff, and Jeff's sister's brother were traveling farther down into Mexico than they had originally planned. Jeff's cousin had met with them on the border the previous day with some chairs but they were not what Bill wanted. When the accident happened, they were returning late at night from a prison that made the chairs that Bill wanted. This prison was located much farther into the interior of the country than he had hoped to go. On the return trip from deep in Mexico, they were hit head-on by a fifth wheel truck. The Mexican police found a business card at the scene and called the Blue Goose. It was only by coincidence that an employee knew my maiden name and they were able to contact my father first so that he could tell me. There are no words to describe how overwhelmed I was and in total disbelief and devastated, to say the least. Once again, however, as when I was in the car accident, my family and friends rallied around me and I had scarce little time to do anything but move forward. McKinley was my reason for getting up and out of bed in the morning and I was so thankful for her. She had been born seven weeks early for no apparent reason, but now I knew she had come early to spend a little more time with her father before he was taken away. Life moved forward and my parents swooped in and were a huge help to us.

McKinley at just four months old and I persevered. We moved to a duplex closer to Mom and Dad. I moved through that first year like a robot. I actually have very little memory of it. My routine was a blur of daycare, work, home, baby, and never being quite sure if I was doing even one of them right. But life moved forward and my daughter was growing and thriving. She was my joy.

Becoming a mother was something I had always dreamed of and in 1992 I became one. I had a deep desire to give birth and go through all of the emotions that I knew my birthmother had experienced. Pregnancy was a wonderful experience for me, the nine months (well, seven and a half months for me as she was seven weeks premature) of feeling a baby growing inside of you. Experiencing all of the joy, fears, anxiety, and unknowns a pregnancy holds. I wanted to see a reflection of me probably more than most because I had no genetic history to base it on.

I personally do not think that I could have ever given a child up for adoption—the bond is so strong that I cannot help but think it would alter your life in some way or another. It would take such strength to go on with life when that bond is abruptly severed. I admire Stacia for her strength.

McKinley is now twenty-two years old and is a beautiful, smart young woman with a bright future ahead of her. I was blessed with a daughter that is more of a realist than I have ever been. She has a good head on her shoulders and I could not be more pleased. I wonder how that happens? I like to think that I gave her the tools she needed to become the incredible young woman that she is today, but who knows. McKinley may have been born premature, but that's where she abandoned that word. She is and has been from day one, the most mature and responsible child I have ever met. She is my biggest joy and will probably never know, unless she goes through something similar in her life, how she truly saved my life. I am so proud of her and wish her a long and healthy life.

Chapter 12
Another Happy Beginning

The neighbors to the right of my parents' lake house at Cedar Creek Lake near Gun Barrel City, Texas are dear, sweet people whom I knew back then, but not very well. They ran a very successful family business selling airplane parts in Dallas. About a year and a half after losing Bill, I got a call from one of their daughters. The call came totally out of the blue and she told me that there was a "single" metal salesman that called on them at their business that they were all crazy about. She had given him my phone number and she wanted us to go out on a date. I was mortified. I had, I guess, thought that part of my life was over. That salesman turned out to be Mike Hendrix. Mike called me, as I am sure he was instructed to do. We spoke very easily for a long time on the phone and discussed the usual "get to know you" small talk that takes place when becoming acquainted with someone new. It was not until after we hung up that I kept repeating Mike's birthday in my head and wondering why that date sounded so familiar. Mike's birthday is February 11, the same day Bill was killed. A friend of mine thought that was creepy, but I chose to think of it as an ending and a new beginning.

I knew at that point that I had begun to turn a corner in my life. Our date was arranged and I remember just wanting to get it over with to appease this well-meaning family. I was excited, but at the same time afraid of something new. This was the way I felt, of course, prior to my meeting the incredible man who picked me up that evening. He was so delightful. I picked the restaurant but on the cautionary side, had a friend of mine, Jim Grant, who played the bass guitar for the Five Americans, planted and sitting at the bar to give me a ride home should the date not go well. I just didn't know what to expect and was scared to death. It just so happened that we ran into his ex-wife while at the restaurant. One would think that in a city the size of Dallas, the odds of that happening were small, but then this was becoming a kind of modus operandi with me.

Mike and I had our first adventure that night and both knew then that we were on to something. He said one of two things were going to happen. "We will look back on this and laugh one day, or this is going the to be worst date each of us has ever had," he commented. Long story short, Mike and I were married nine months later. He gave me and McKinley a new life. We became a happy family of four. I am so grateful to Mike and his son Wes Hendrix for the family we have become. Wes moved in with us shortly after our marriage. He was twelve years older than McKinley and he handled her like he had been around a two and a half year old all of his life. He was so good with her and she adored him. We laughed because Wes started college at Texas A&M University the day McKinley started kindergarten. Time flies. It has been an awesome and adventurous twenty years. I am so proud of my family.

Adoption seemed to be a recurring theme in my life. Mike legally adopted McKinley when she was five. It was a wonderful moment for all of us and we celebrated with a party. McKinley knew of my adoption and she thought it perfectly normal for someone to have two sets of parents, grandparents, and other relatives. But once again, so-called "well meaning people"can be cruel when talking about adoption. I remember McKinley coming home when she was in the second grade being very upset. For the "all about me" day in class, where students were assigned a day when they would tell their classmates all about themselves, she had chosen to tell her adoption story and about her big brother Wessy being in college. McKinley adored and idolized Wessy, which was the name she chose for him at two and a half years old and still uses when referring to her brother today. After completing her little speech on her assigned day, the teacher, of all people, told her that she hoped McKinley was aware and understood that Wes was not really her brother, but that he was ONLY her stepbrother. This one teacher's thoughtless comment to a little girl was very confusing to her and contradicted what Mike and I had told her. Mike and I explained that the teacher was talking about Wes being a biological brother and that just deepened her confusion. We reassured her that Wes certainly was and always would be her brother in her heart. She seemed to be okay with that but I was furious with that teacher. These were thoughtless words spoken to a child that were not necessary. Think before you speak was a good lesson for all of us.

Chapter 13
Finding — and Losing — Bruce

My husband met my biological father for the first time when we all flew to Nebraska to visit Bruce and my sister Pam. When Mike saw him at the airport he simply said, "Oh, my God—you look just like him." Enough said. It made me so happy.

What a wild visit that trip to Nebraska was. We learned that Bruce owned a biker bar, named Kitty's Place. However, on this first trip with my family in tow, we went to every bar but his. He told Mike later that Kitty's Place was a little too rough; we would visit that one the next time. Bruce and his entourage drank a lot and much of the winter life in Hastings, Nebraska, seemed to take place in the bars. Everyone knew him and it was the kind of little town where the old guys sit and re-play, through stories, the "game winning catch" so-and-so made back in 19-something. They relived the games over and over again, almost as if they were predicting the future or could change the outcome. Bruce seemed very happy in his element and he was well liked. Mike and I noticed that there would always be one of the special drinks he called his "iced tea" (Seagram's VO Canadian whiskey and iced tea, way before it became popular) waiting for him on the bar when he walked in.

Bruce introduced me as his daughter everywhere we went. It made me feel very welcome and so happy that he seemed so proud to introduce me this way. I am also quite sure that it made juicy fodder for a lot of good gossip. His sense of humor was right on point. Mike, the best joke teller I know, and Bruce went toe to toe, each one trying to top the other's joke during the whole visit. To showcase his sense of humor, I learned that Bruce owned a concrete company at one point and the logo on the side of the trucks read "Edwards Concrete, Everything We Touch Gets Hard." I learned that after his football career he went on to own racecars, was a very successful gambler, a politician, business owner, and a farmer.

Before we left Nebraska, Bruce told Mike that if anything ever happened to him, he wanted Mike to be sure and come get his vacuum cleaner. Mike thought that a strange request and simply said, "Well, okay then." Bruce later told Mike in private over the phone that his vacuum cleaner bag was where he held large sums of money. Gambling winnings is how he described it, then he belly laughed and proclaimed that it had certainly NEVER been used to clean anything!

My mom and dad, Ben and Betty, had a lovely lake house at Cedar Creek Lake. They were invited to and attended a Super Bowl party given by some lake neighbors. I had just recently found and made contact with Bruce and at one point during the gathering my mom started telling the group the story of my search for my biological parents. She tells the story very well. She said that there was one couple in attendance that they did not know very well and they excused themselves right in the middle of her story and left. The couple returned shortly with a high school yearbook in hand. The gentleman and his wife began telling the crowd that they, too, were from Hastings, Nebraska, and had been classmates in high school with Bruce. After hearing the beginnings of Betty's story they had gone home to retrieve the yearbook with his picture. Betty and Ben had no idea the couple was from Nebraska. What are the odds of such a random coincidence? They also confirmed the stories I had heard of his popularity and talent as an athlete—his raucous ways, but said he was a well-liked and fun guy.

Sadly, Bruce was diagnosed with throat cancer in 2001 and passed away on September 25, 2003. I had many good years and countless phone conversations with him that I will treasure always. I had found my father. I will never forget the feeling I got when staring into his eyes, it was like looking into my own eyes. It is an experience I will always treasure.

Chapter 14
Kinship and Friendship

Stacia had been correct in telling me that Bruce would not remember her. He did not. He even went to the Hastings College Archives and looked at pictures. Bruce explained to me that was a wild time in his life. In 1955 he was making a large salary and had a lot of money after signing with a pro-football team and, apparently, a lot of women too. Bruce told me he even called Stacia at one point and they conversed. He played football at Hastings College with the famed Tom Osborne, who was a freshman quarterback when Bruce was a senior. They became friends and Osborne, of course, became an all-time winning coach for the University of Nebraska from 1973 to 1997, and later a U.S. Representative for the Third Congressional District from 2001 to 2007. Osborne visited Bruce towards the end of his fight with cancer, which I found touching. In 1957 Bruce was drafted by and played for the Canadian Tiger Cats, and was then drafted by the Washington Redskins where he played a short while. He was inducted into the Hastings College Football Hall of Fame in 1999. This was a big honor for him and I was so very proud for him.

I was happy in finding Bruce and in the end, it didn't matter to me that he could not recall what had happened. Nevertheless, Bruce told me he felt like he needed to make up for lost time. It seemed to really bother him. This was not at all the way I felt; he owed me nothing and I made that clear. We did resemble each other and I relished that.

My relationship with Stacia is ongoing. She currently lives in Houston. We speak on the phone and remember birthdays and holidays through cards. She is always kind and we discuss all kind of things. She is always happy to answer any questions I may have. I am happy that I found my biological mother.

A few years ago I received a phone call from Stacia. She said that she had told her son, Cam, the truth about our relationship, and he had taken it very well. I am so happy that times have changed and I think that she was probably relieved to have that burden from her past lifted, if that was what it was to her. We still visit from time to time. I think that she has chosen to treat our relationship in a very matter of fact manner. What had happened in the past had happened. We are very realistic about it and have no expectations. We both live our lives and understand our relationship. The old saying "it is what it is" always comes to my mind when I think of the circumstances. I had set a goal and I accomplished that goal, but more importantly, I learned so much along the way. I am very proud of that.

Ironically, my friend Richard is currently Stacia's neighbor in Houston and sees Stacia in her front yard on a regular basis when he is out riding the neighborhood on his Harley. They have struck up a kind of friendship through me and Richard always calls to let me know how she is and what's going on. I find it so amusing to think that a friend I met at college would play such a pivotal role in my search. I could not ever have dreamed that my story would play out this way.

I realize, of course, that it was a different world in the 1950s. Unwed mothers were ostracized and I truly admire Stacia for the courage it must have taken her as a young woman to leave her home and her state, to start a new life, and I mean that literally—mine and hers. I know that she was not the first woman this had happened to, nor will she be the last, but it was a burden for me as a child to think that I might have ruined someone's life and caused so much pain and/or resentment.

My search has helped me understand that I had always felt guilty, not so much for being born, but knowing that someone, a stranger somewhere, had been forced by society to change her course in life because of me. Searching for and finding out the truth led me to the realization that I had nothing to do with it. The decisions she made, I am grateful for and I thank her. In the end all of the choices we as flawed humans make, the good, the bad and the ugly, have consequences. In life, I have finally realized that another choice in life is to own any achievement, failure, or wrongdoing. Choose to accept it, be proud and pat yourself on the back, or forgive yourself or someone you might have wronged and move forward, whatever it takes—and to love like there is no tomorrow. I like a quote I recently came across by Dr. Albert Einstein:

> *I know quite certainly that I myself have*
> *no special talents; curiosity, obsession*
> *and dogged endurance, combined with*
> *self-criticism, have brought me to my ideas.*

Chapter 15
Reflections on Who I Am

Growing up "Bowden" meant that we were all familiar with a little catch phrase. The little string of words was "remember who you are." I grew up hearing it over and over again. I have been told that the phrase originated in my father's family and was often expressed to someone as they were leaving the house. The phrase was meant, by my interpretation, to remind you to always be on your best behavior, not to do anything to embarrass yourself or the family, to always maintain a good reputation, and most of all to always retain your self-respect and integrity. I used to laugh and mostly cringe upon hearing this when leaving the house. It seemed I always had to explain the utterance to whomever was with me and they would generally just give me a blank stare and shrug their shoulders. When I was young I assumed that all families did something similar and what I thought back then to be quite silly.

It wasn't until I was much older that I realized that the phrase was something that I always carried with me. The words were embedded in me and would pop into my head at various times in my life for no good reason -- or so I thought. I can recall many times that the phrase made me stop and rethink some of my choices, maybe just for a split second.. I usually did not like this subconscious little reminder. It was like having the little angel on one shoulder and the devil on the other. But looking back, I am so grateful for those words.

As an adult, and I swore I would not do this, I find myself reciting the phrase often. I include it as a postscript on most cards and notes that I write as "RWYA" (Remember Who You Are) to my kids, my husband, and, of course, myself. It is a powerful, compact message reminding the recipient of love and self-awareness—and it packs a powerful psychological punch.

In retrospect, I think that little phrase motivated me to seek and find out who I really was. I had been told all of my life to "remember who you are," but who was I, really? I found this to be ironic.

It has now been some years since my search and as I reflect back I now realize that I knew who I was all along. But searching for and finding out the truth about my biological makeup just made that "me" a better, more caring, feeling, compassionate, and self-assured "me." The journey taught me new strengths and weaknesses I had not fully known. In my case, finding my biological parents grounded me. The confidence and self-awareness I learned along the way and finally knowing the truth made my foundation strong and provided me with a calmness that I cannot put into words.

This brings me full circle back to my mother's letter and her original question: Does environment make the child or does our genetic makeup trump that? I believe that in my case, through luck of the draw, it was the best of both worlds that made, shaped, and guided me into the person that I am today. I feel the need to share this information for several reasons. I know that mine is an interesting story showing once again that truth is more often than not stranger than fiction. My search yielded a good outcome and for that I am so grateful, but I know that is not always the case. Bruce's daughter, my adopted sister, searched for and found her biological parents and it was not a pleasant outcome. I do believe that it deeply hurt her. I want to help inspire and/or caution someone who may be struggling whether or not to make the decision to search or not search for biological parents or children. There are no guarantees and you just never know what the results might be.

The original purpose of my search was to learn about my biological parents, but in the end, it was myself that I learned far more about. The decision to search was the right decision for me. As the great scientist and humanitarian Dr. Linus Pauling said, "Satisfaction of one's curiosity is one of the greatest sources of happiness in life."

Birth Father Bruce Edwards - In the Service in California in 1953.

Stacia's Career as a Nurse

Stacia Coryell
Birthmother

Stacia

Bruce Edwards - Athlete

One cannot talk about the great players in Bronco football history without mentioning the name of Bruce Edwards. Bruce played for the Broncos during the 1950, 1954 and 1955 seasons. In each of these years impact and contributions to the team were significant.

An outstanding halfback and kicker, Bruce led the team in scoring in each of the three seasons he played and he was the State of Nebraska scoring champion in both 1954 and 1955. In 1954 he scored 13 touchdowns and kicked 13 extra points and his 91 total points scored ranked him sixth in scoring in all small colleges in the nation.

Many adjectives were used to describe Bruce Edwards during his playing days. He was known as a "blazing bronco back" a "slashing halfback" and "a bruising runner that at times is almost impossible to stop" and it was stated, he "seems to have a nose for the end zone."

His kicking skills were also significant and many local fans still talk about his booming kicks.

One person in support of Bruce's consideration for this honor commented: "even when considering the present increased size of today's athlete and the advantages of modern-day facilities and equipment and coaching, Bruce would have been the starting running back on any of the recently fielded teams at Hastings College.

Bruce Edwards was named to both All Conference and All State teams while at Hastings College. His skills and level of play have earned him a spot in the Hastings College Athletic Hall of Fame.

Write-up used in Bruce's Hall of Fame ceremony at Hastings College.

Bev and Bruce - 2002

Husband Mike and Bruce

Bev and McKinley kissing Bruce in 2002.

Half-brother Cameron and Stacia in 2008.

Alice Erickson, Bruce Edwards and McKinley Hendrix

Bev, Mike and Bruce on the patio in Dallas in 2003.

Bev, Bruce and McKinley in Nebraska in 2002.

Bev, Bruce and Bruce's adopted daughter, Pam in Nebraska in 1997.

About the Author

Bev was born in Dallas, Texas in 1956. She was adopted at three days old by Ben and Betty Bowden and raised in a loving home with two brothers that were also adopted. After three adoptions, Ben and Betty had two biological sons of their own that were born in 1962 and 1963, giving her a total of four brothers. Good fortune was on her side to be adopted by Dr. Ben and Betty Bowden. She was a part of a glorious blended family that she is so thankful for.

She attended Bryan Adams High School in Dallas and received her B.S. in design, merchandising and marketing from the University of North Texas in 1978.

In 1984, Bev was given the support by her family which came in the form of a heart felt letter from her mother, Betty, giving Bev her blessing to search for and to fulfill the always-present question in her life to seek out her birth parents. She began the journey to attempt to find answers to many of the questions that come with being adopted. Even in the best possible scenario of adoption, which was hers, there are always the nagging questions of who am I, where did I come from, and why did you not want me.

Bev is recently retired after twenty-eight years in legal field in Dallas, Texas where she was fortunate enough to live with her stepson Wes Hendrix, an amazing young man she is so proud of and her and Mike's beautiful daughter, McKinley Hendrix. Bev currently lives with her husband Mike at their beautiful new log home on their ranch they call "Two Bucks" in Rochelle, Texas.

www.ingramcontent.com/pod-product-compliance
Lightning Source LLC
LaVergne TN
LVHW051528070426
835507LV00023B/3362